CW00500147

AIR FRYER RECIPES

Quick and Appetizing Recipes for Cooking Light in Many Ways

EASY EDITION

© Copyright 2021 - All rights reserved.
The content contained within this book may not be reproduced, duplicated or transmitted without direct written permission from the author or the publisher.

Under no circumstances will any blame or legal responsibility be held against the publisher, or author, for any damages, reparation, or monetary loss due to the information contained within this book. Either directly or indirectly.

Legal Notice:

This book is copyright protected. This book is only for personal use. You cannot amend, distribute, sell, use, quote or paraphrase any part, or the content within this book, without the consent of the author or publisher.

Disclaimer Notice:

Please note the information contained within this document is for educational and entertainment purposes only. All effort has been executed to present accurate, up to date, and reliable, complete information. No warranties of any kind are declared or implied. Readers acknowledge that the author is not engaging in the rendering of legal, financial, medical or professional advice. The content within this book has been derived from various sources. Please consult a licensed professional before attempting any techniques outlined in this book.

By reading this document, the reader agrees that under no circumstances is the author responsible for any losses, direct or indirect, which are incurred as a result of the use of information contained within this document, including, but not limited to, errors, omissions, or inaccuracies.

Table of Contents

Sommario

TABLE OF CONTENTS 5

INTRODUCTION 7

What is an air fryer? 7
How do air fryers work? 7
Here are the thanks for using an air fryer: 7
What are you ready to cook in an air fryer? 8
Air fryer tips 9

CHICKEN 11

Hot Chicken Drumettes with Peppers 12
Southwest Buttermilk Chicken Thighs 14
Grandma's Chicken with Rosemary and Sweet Potatoes 15
Mediterranean Chicken Breasts with Roasted Tomatoes 17
Traditional Chicken Teriyaki 18
The Best Chicken Burgers Ever 20

PORK 21

Perfect Pork Wraps 22
Caprese Pork Chops 24
Asian Sticky Ribs 25
Pork Koftas with Yoghurt Sauce 27
Ranchero Pork Kebabs 28
Cheesy Creamy Pork Casserole 30

BEEF 31

Kansas City-Style Ribs 32
Beef Parmigiana Sliders 34
Beef and Sausage Meatloaf with Peppers 35
Birthday Party Cheeseburger Pizza 37
Kid-Friendly Mini Meatloaves 38
Steak Fingers with Lime Sauce 40

FISH 41

Famous Tuna Niçoise Salad 42
Greek-Style Sea Bass 44
Halibut Steak with Zoodles and Lemon 46
Roasted Mediterranean Snapper Fillets 47
Quick-Fix Seafood Breakfast 49
Shrimp Scampi Dip with Cheese 50

VEGETABLE AND SIDE DISHES 51

Hot Mexican Corn on the Cob 52
Mexican-Style Roasted Zucchini 54

Favorite Winter Bliss Bowl 55
Classic Onion Rings 56
Cauliflower and Goat Cheese Croquettes 58
Tater Tot Vegetable Casserole 60

SNACKS & APPETIZERS 61

Beer-Battered Vidalia Onion Rings 62
Pepper and Bacon Mini Skewers 64
Hot Paprika Bacon Deviled Eggs 65
Quick and Easy Popcorn 67
Hot Cheesy Mushrooms Bites 69
Sea Scallops and Bacon Skewers 71

RICE AND GRAIN 73

Chocolate Chip Bread Pudding Squares 74
Italian-Style Fried Polenta Slices 76
Beef Taquito Casserole 77
Ciabatta Bread Pudding with Walnuts 79
Paella-Style Spanish Rice 81
Air Grilled Cheese Roll-Ups 82

VEGAN 83

Decadent Carrot Salad with Sultanas 84
Authentic Platanos Maduros 85
Spicy Sesame Cauliflower Steaks 87
Traditional Indian Pakora 89
Barbecue Tofu with Green Beans 91
Polish Placki Ziemniaczan 92

DESSERT 94

Crunchy French Toast Sticks 95
Old-Fashioned Baked Pears 97
Chocolate Puff Pastry Sticks 99
Nana's Famous Apple Fritters 101
The Ultimate Berry Crumble 103
Old-Fashioned Baked Pears 105

OTHER AIR FRYER 107

Chicken Burgers 108
Chicken Nuggets and Turnip Chips 110
Fried pork ribs 112
Chuck Roast in sweet sauce 114
Simple burgers 116
Cod fillets 118
Mediterranean broccoli 120
Greek zucchini 122
Greek Tiganites 124
Chocolate cake 126

Introduction

What is an air fryer?

An air fryer is an amplified countertop convection oven. The small device claims to mimic the results of frying with hot air and little or no oil.

This gadget has increased in popularity over the past few years. There are all kinds of things you'll air fry, from frozen chicken wings and homemade fries to roasted vegetables and freshly baked cookies.

How do air fryers work?

The top section of an air fryer contains a heating mechanism and a fan. You place your food during a fryer-style basket and once it's turned on, hot air rushes down and around the food. This rapid circulation makes the food crispy - much like frying, but without the oil.

Here are the thanks for using an air fryer:

1. Place your food inside the basket.
Depending on the size of your air fryer, the basket can hold anywhere from 2 to 10 liters. In most cases, you'll want to put in 1 or 2 teaspoons of oil to help your food get nice and crispy.

2. Set the time and temperature

Air fryer cooking times and temperatures typically range from 5 to 25 minutes at 350° to 400°F, depending on the food you're cooking.

3. Let the food cookIn some cases, you'll need to flip the food halfway through the cooking time to help it crisp up evenly. Once you're done cooking, it's important to wipe down the air fryer.

What are you ready to cook in an air fryer?

While many of the unique recipes using an air fryer are typically fried foods, you'll also use this appliance to roast vegetables, cook meat, and bake cookies.

Frozen Finger Foods
The air fryer could also be a star when it comes to preparing frozen foods that are meant to taste fried. Frozen fries, mozzarella sticks, and chicken nuggets are a variety of frozen fried foods you can make.

Homemade Finger Foods
If you prefer to form your finger foods from scratch, the air fryer could also be an excellent option for creating homemade crispy snacks and side dishes: try Air-Fryer Sweet Potato Fries, Air-Fryer Pickles, or Air-Fryer Papas Rellenas.

Chicken, fish, and meat
Air-fryers aren't just for greasy carbs-you can also make protein-packed dishes. Try chicken recipes with an air fryer, like Nashville Hot Chicken. For a healthier option, Air-Fryer Keto Meatballs are a superb choice. When it comes to fish and seafood dishes, we love this Air-Fryer Crumb-Covered Sole.

Roasted Vegetables

Because air fryers are essentially small convection ovens, they're great for roasting vegetables, especially if you're only cooking for one or two people. A variety of our favorite air fryer vegetable recipes include herbed and lemon cauliflower and garlic and rosemary Brussels sprouts.
However, when using this gadget to cook vegetables, skip the leafy greens.

Some foods
Air fryers are often great for creating single-serving desserts, including foods as small as cookies and apple fritters (here are the thanks for making cookies with an air fryer). you'll also try making these mint lava cakes for the winter vacations or these mini Nutella donut holes from the air fryer for an indulgent treat any time of year.
However, you can't make anything that uses a liquid batter (unless you freeze it first).

Air fryer tips

Is air-fried food healthy?
You could argue that air-fried food is healthier than fried food because it uses less oil. Frozen fries prepared with an air fryer contain between 4 and 6 grams of fat compared to their fried counterparts, which have as much as 17 grams per serving.

Air fryers make it easy to prepare frozen foods, and they will do so in a way that is healthier than frying. The results are much better than oven frying, and your kitchen stays fresh.

Even the most prominent air fryers have a limited capacity, so you're likely to have to cook in batches, especially if you're preparing food for a crowd. Larger than a toaster, air fryers also take up valuable counter space. Finally, they will be expensive, depending on the model you get.

With numerous models on the market, this popular appliance has dropped in price within the previous few years-many models cost but $200 and a couple of cost but $100.

In any case, the advantages of owning an air fryer are many

Chicken

Hot Chicken Drumettes with Peppers

(Ready in about 45 minutes | Servings 3)

397 Calories; 18.8g Fat; 20.6g Carbs; 34.2g Protein; 3.1g Sugars

Ingredients

1/2 cup all-purpose four
1 teaspoon kosher salt
1 teaspoon shallot powder
1/2 teaspoon dried basil
1/2 teaspoon dried oregano
1/2 teaspoon smoked paprika
1 tablespoon hot sauce
1/4 cup mayonnaise
1/4 cup milk
1 pound chicken drumettes
2 bell peppers, sliced

Directions

In a shallow bowl, mix the flour, salt, shallot powder, basil, oregano and smoked paprika.
In another bowl, mix the hot sauce, mayonnaise and milk.
Dip the chicken drumettes in the flour mixture, then, coat them with the milk mixture; make sure to coat well on all sides.
Cook in the preheated Air Fryer at 380 degrees F for 28 to 30 minutes; turn them over halfway through the cooking time. Reserve chicken drumettes, keeping them warm.
Then, cook the peppers at 400 degrees F for 13 to 15 minutes, shaking the basket once or twice. Eat warm.

Southwest Buttermilk Chicken Thighs

(Ready in about 15 minutes + marinating time | Servings 2)

449 Calories; 12g Fat; 33.4g Carbs; 49g Protein; 8.5g Sugars

Ingredients

1 pound chicken thighs
1 cup buttermilk
1/2 teaspoon garlic paste
1/4 cup Sriracha sauce
Sea salt and ground black pepper, to taste
1 teaspoon cayenne pepper
1/4 cup cornflour
1/4 cup all-purpose flour

Directions

Pat dry the chicken thighs with kitchen towels.
Now, thoroughly combine the buttermilk, garlic paste, Sriracha sauce, salt, black pepper and cayenne pepper.
Dredge the chicken into the mixture until well coated. Place in your refrigerator for 2 hours.
Place the flour in another shallow bowl. Coat the chicken thigs with the flour mixture.
Cook in your Air Fryer at 395 degrees F for 12 minutes. Bon appétit!

Grandma's Chicken with Rosemary and Sweet Potatoes

(Ready in about 35 minutes | Servings 2)

604 Calories; 36.1g Fat; 23.4g Carbs; 44.5g Protein; 2.5g Sugars

Ingredients

2 chicken legs, bone-in
2 garlic cloves, minced
1 teaspoon sesame oil
2 Sea salt and ground black pepper, to taste
3 sprigs rosemary, leaves picked and crushed
1/2 pound sweet potatoes

Directions

Start by preheating your Air Fryer to 380 degrees F. Now, rub garlic halves all over the chicken legs.

Drizzle the chicken legs and sweet potatoes with the sesame oil. Sprinkle them with salt and rosemary. Place the chicken and potatoes in the cooking basket.

Cook in the preheated Air Fryer for 30 minutes until the potatoes are thoroughly cooked. The chicken must reach an internal temperature of 165 degrees F.

Serve the chicken legs garnished with the sweet potatoes. Bon appétit!

Mediterranean Chicken Breasts with Roasted Tomatoes

(Ready in about 1 hour | Servings 8)

315 Calories; 17.1g Fat; 2.7g Carbs; 36g Protein; 1.7g Sugars

Ingredients

1 teaspoons olive oil, melted
2 pounds chicken breasts, bone-in
1/2 teaspoon black pepper, freshly ground
1/2 teaspoon salt
1 teaspoon cayenne pepper
2 tablespoons fresh parsley, minced
1 teaspoon fresh basil, minced
1 teaspoon fresh rosemary, minced
4 medium-sized Roma tomatoes, halved

Directions

Start by preheating your Air Fryer to 370 degrees F. Brush the cooking basket with 1 teaspoon of olive oil.
Sprinkle the chicken breasts with all seasonings listed above.
Cook for 25 minutes or until chicken breasts are slightly browned. Work in batches.
Arrange the tomatoes in the cooking basket and brush them with the remaining teaspoon of olive oil. Season with sea salt.
Cook the tomatoes at 350 degrees F for 10 minutes, shaking halfway through the cooking time.
Serve with chicken breasts. Bon appétit!

Traditional Chicken Teriyaki

(Ready in about 50 minutes | Servings 4)

362 Calories; 21.1g Fat; 4.4g Carbs; 36.6g Protein; 2.4g Sugars

Ingredients

1 ½ pounds chicken breast, halved
1 tablespoon lemon juice
2 tablespoons Mirin
1/4 cup milk
2 tablespoons soy sauce
1 tablespoon olive oil
1 teaspoon ginger, peeled and grated
2 garlic cloves, minced
1/2 teaspoon salt
1/2 teaspoon ground black pepper
1 teaspoon cornstarch

Directions

In a large ceramic dish, place the chicken, lemon juice, Mirin, milk, soy sauce, olive oil, ginger, and garlic. Let it marinate for 30 minutes in your refrigerator.
Spritz the sides and bottom of the cooking basket with a nonstick cooking spray. Arrange the chicken in the cooking basket and cook at 370 degrees F for 10 minutes.
Turn over the chicken, baste with the reserved marinade and cook for 4 minutes longer. Taste for doneness, season with salt and pepper, and reserve.
Mix the cornstarch with 1 tablespoon of water. Add the marinade to the preheated skillet over medium heat; cook for 3 to 4 minutes. Now, stir in the cornstarch slurry and cook until the sauce thickens. Spoon the sauce over the reserved chicken and serve immediately.

The Best Chicken Burgers Ever

(Ready in about 20 minutes | Servings 4)

507 Calories; 26.5g Fat; 37.6g Carbs; 30g Protein; 12.8g Sugars

Ingredients

1 tablespoon olive oil
1 onion, peeled and finely chopped
2 garlic cloves, minced
Sea salt and ground black pepper, to taste
1/2 teaspoon paprika
1/2 teaspoon ground cumin
1 pound chicken breast, ground
4 soft rolls
4 tablespoons ketchup
4 tablespoons mayonnaise
2 teaspoons Dijon mustard
4 tablespoons green onions, chopped
4 pickles, sliced

Directions

Heat the olive oil in a skillet over high flame. Then, sauté the onion until golden and translucent, about 4 minutes.
Add the garlic and cook an additional 30 seconds or until it is aromatic. Season with salt, pepper, paprika, and cumin; reserve.
Add the chicken and cook for 2 to 3 minutes, stirring and crumbling with a fork. Add the onion mixture and mix to combine well.
Shape the mixture into patties and transfer them to the cooking basket. Cook in the preheated Air Fryer at 360 degrees F for 6 minutes. Turn them over and cook an additional 5 minutes. Work in batches.
Smear the base of the roll with ketchup, mayo, and mustard. Top with the chicken, green onions, and pickles. Enjoy!

Pork

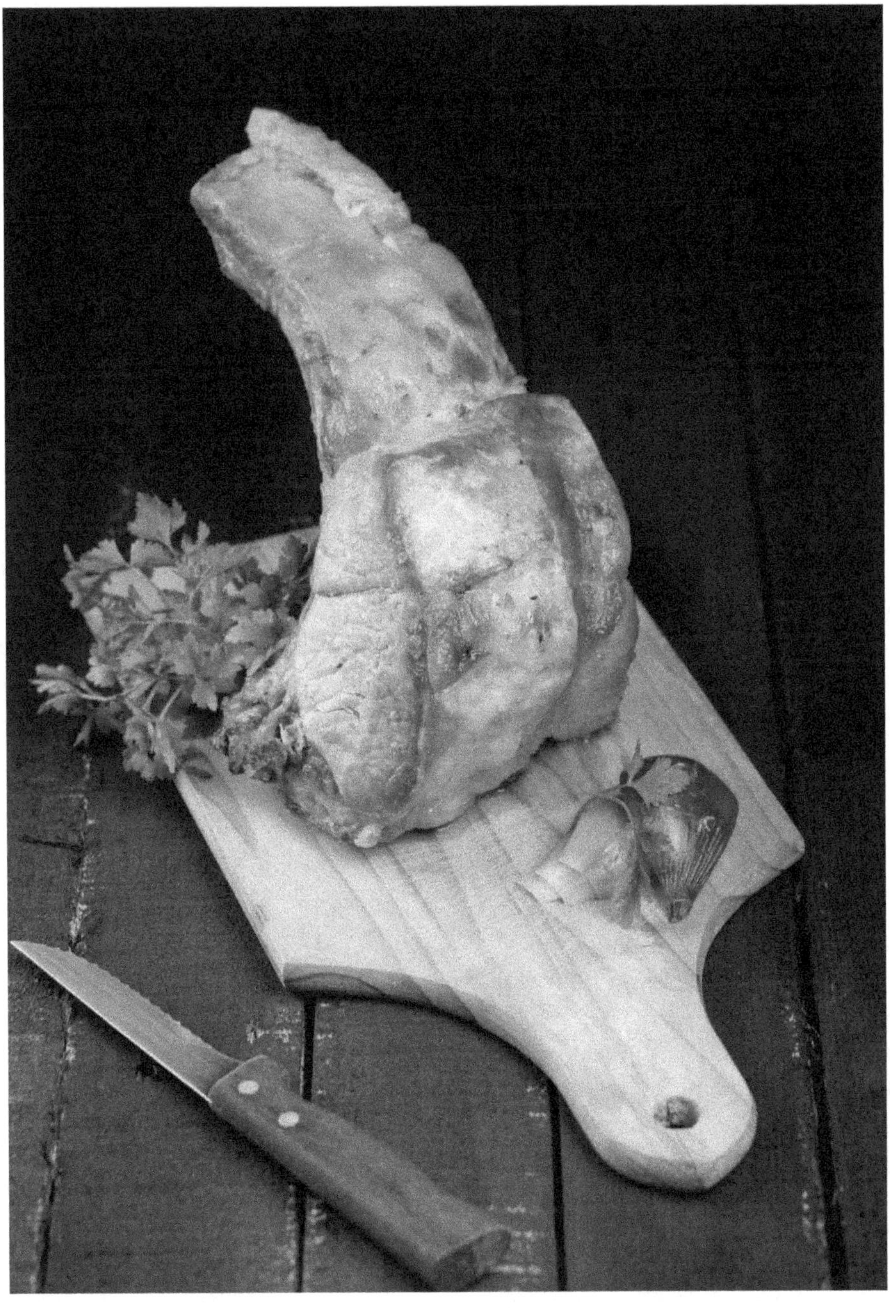

Perfect Pork Wraps

(Ready in about 55 minutes | Servings 2)

558 Calories; 25.7g Fat; 44.1g Carbs; 34.3g Protein; 7.2g Sugars

Ingredients

1/2 pound pork loin
1 teaspoon butter, melted
Salt and black pepper, to season
1/2 teaspoon marjoram
1/2 teaspoon hot paprika
2 tortillas
Sauce:
2 tablespoons tahini
1 tablespoon sesame oil
2 tablespoons soy sauce
1 tablespoon lime juice
1 tablespoon white vinegar
1 teaspoon fresh ginger, peeled and grated
2 garlic cloves, pressed
1 teaspoon honey

Directions

Rub the pork with melted butter and season with salt, pepper, marjoram and hot paprika.
Place in the cooking basket and cook at 360 digress F for 25 minutes. Turn the meat over and cook an additional 20 minutes.
Place the roasted pork loin on a cutting board. Slice the roasted pork loin into strips using a sharp kitchen knife.
In the meantime, mix the sauce ingredients with a wire whisk.
Turn the temperature to 390 degrees F. Spoon the pork strips and sauce onto each tortilla; wrap them tightly.
Drizzle with a nonstick cooking spray and bake about 6 minutes.
Serve warm.

Caprese Pork Chops

(Ready in about 15 minutes + marinating time | Servings 3)

345 Calories; 12.9g Fat; 14.7g Carbs; 40.3g Protein; 10.8g Sugars

Ingredients

1 pound center-cut pork chops, boneless
1/4 cup balsamic vinegar
1 tablespoon honey
1 tablespoon whole-grain mustard
1/2 teaspoon olive oil
1/2 teaspoon smoked paprika
Salt and black pepper, to taste
1/2 teaspoon shallot powder
1/2 teaspoon porcini powder
1/2 teaspoon granulated garlic
3 slices fresh mozzarella
3 thick slices tomatoes
2 tablespoons fresh basil leaves, chopped

Directions

Place the pork chops, balsamic vinegar, honey, mustard, olive oil and spices in a bowl. Cover and let it marinate in your refrigerator for 1 hour.

Cook in the preheated Air Fryer at 400 degrees F for 7 minutes. Top with cheese and continue to cook for 5 minutes more.

Top with sliced tomato and basil and serve immediately.

Asian Sticky Ribs

(Ready in about 40 minutes | Servings 4)

446 Calories; 29.6g Fat; 5.5g Carbs; 45.1g Protein; 4.1g Sugars

Ingredients

1 teaspoon salt
1 teaspoon cayenne pepper
1/2 teaspoon ground black pepper
2 teaspoons raw honey
2 garlic cloves, minced
1 (1-inch) piece ginger, peeled and grated
1/2 teaspoon onion powder
1/2 teaspoon porcini powder
1 teaspoon mustard seeds
1 tablespoon sweet chili sauce
1 tablespoon balsamic vinegar
1 ½ pounds pork country-style ribs

Directions

In a mixing bowl, combine the salt, cayenne pepper, black pepper, honey, garlic, ginger, onion powder, porcini powder, mustard seeds, sweet chili sauce, and balsamic vinegar.

Toss and rub the seasoning mixture all over the pork ribs.

Cook the country-style ribs at 360 degrees F for 15 minutes; flip the ribs and cook an additional 20 minutes or until they are tender inside and crisp on the outside.

Serve warm, garnished with fresh chives if desired.

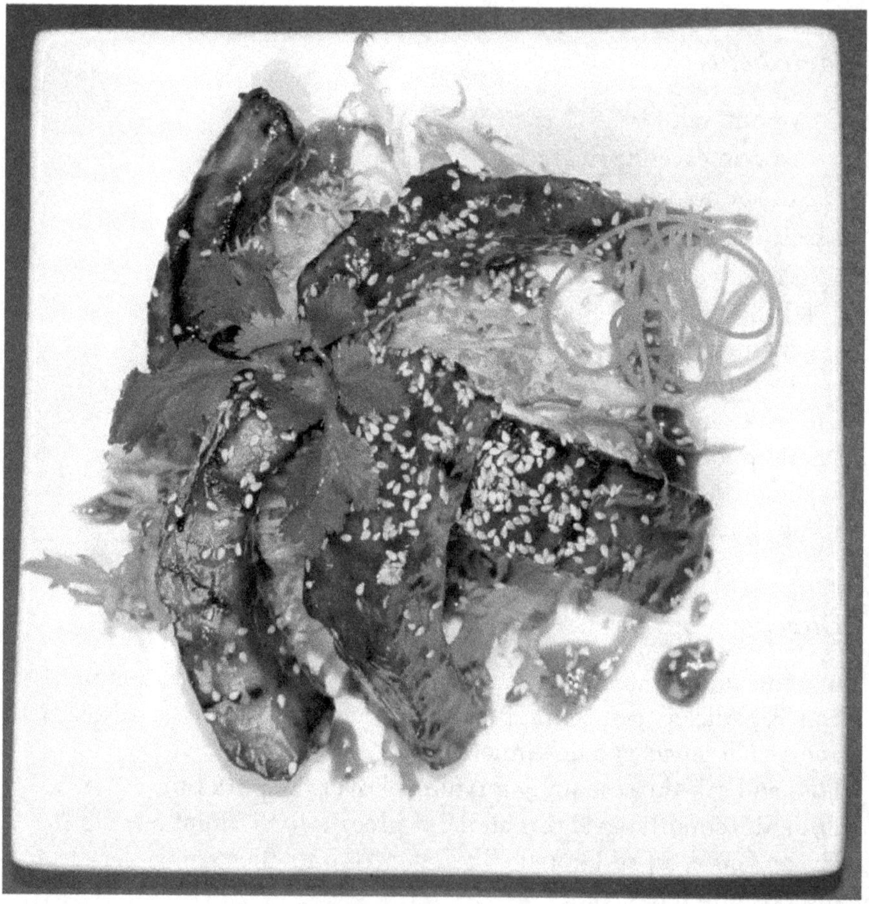

Pork Koftas with Yoghurt Sauce

(Ready in about 25 minutes | Servings 4)

407 Calories; 28.5g Fat; 3.4g Carbs; 32.9g Protein; 1.3g Sugars

Ingredients

2 teaspoons olive oil
1/2 pound ground pork
1/2 pound ground beef
1 egg, whisked
Sea salt and ground black pepper, to taste
1 teaspoon paprika
2 garlic cloves, minced
1 teaspoon dried marjoram
1 teaspoon mustard seeds
1/2 teaspoon celery seeds Yogurt Sauce:
2 tablespoons olive oil
2 tablespoons fresh lemon juice
Sea salt, to taste
1/4 teaspoon red pepper flakes, crushed
1/2 cup full-fat yogurt
1 teaspoon dried dill weed

Directions

Spritz the sides and bottom of the cooking basket with 2 teaspoons of olive oil.

In a mixing dish, thoroughly combine the ground pork, beef, egg, salt, black pepper, paprika, garlic, marjoram, mustard seeds, and celery seeds.

Form the mixture into kebabs and transfer them to the greased cooking basket. Cook at 365 degrees F for 11 to 12 minutes, turning them over once or twice.

In the meantime, mix all the sauce ingredients and place in the refrigerator until ready to serve.

Serve the pork koftas with the yogurt sauce on the side. Enjoy!

Ranchero Pork Kebabs

(Ready in about 25 minutes | Servings 3)

394 Calories; 16.7g Fat; 32.9g Carbs; 29.1g Protein; 4.9g Sugars

Ingredients

1 pound lean pork, ground
1 onion, chopped
1 garlic clove, smashed
1 teaspoon mustard
Salt and ground black pepper, to taste
4 tablespoons ranch-flavored tortilla chips, finely crushed

Directions

Mix all ingredients using your hands. Knead until everything is well incorporated.
Shape the meat mixture around flat skewers (sausage shapes).
Cook at 365 degrees F for 11 to 12 minutes, turning them over once or twice. Work in batches. Serve!

Cheesy Creamy Pork Casserole

(Ready in about 25 minutes | Servings 4)

433 Calories; 20.4g Fat; 2.6g Carbs; 56.5g Protein; 0.3g Sugars

Ingredients

2 tablespoons olive oil
2 pounds pork tenderloin, cut into serving-size pieces
1 teaspoon coarse sea salt
1/2 teaspoon freshly ground pepper
1/4 teaspoon chili powder
1 teaspoon dried marjoram
1 tablespoon mustard
1 cup Ricotta cheese
1 ½ cups chicken broth

Directions

Start by preheating your Air Fryer to 350 degrees F.
Heat the olive oil in a pan over medium-high heat. Once hot, cook the pork for 6 to 7 minutes, flipping it to ensure even cooking.
Arrange the pork in a lightly greased casserole dish. Season with salt, black pepper, chili powder, and marjoram.
In a mixing dish, thoroughly combine the mustard, cheese, and chicken broth. Pour the mixture over the pork chops in the casserole dish.
Bake for another 15 minutes or until bubbly and heated through.
Bon appétit!

Beef

Kansas City-Style Ribs

(Ready in about 35 minutes + marinating time | Servings 3)

327 Calories; 13.4g Fat; 9.2g Carbs; 32.4g Protein; 6.9g Sugars

Ingredients

1 pound beef ribs
1/4 cup ketchup
1/4 cup rum
1 tablespoon mustard
1 tablespoon olive oil
1 tablespoon brown sugar
1 teaspoon garlic powder
1/2 teaspoon onion powder
1/2 teaspoon chili powder
1 teaspoon liquid smoke
Sea salt and ground black pepper, to season

Directions

Place all ingredients in a ceramic bowl, cover and allow it to marinate for 3 to 4 hours.
Roast in your Air Fryer at 400 degrees F for 10 minutes. Reduce heat to 330 degrees F and cook an additional 20 minutes.
Warm the remaining marinade in a nonstick skillet over a moderate flame to make the sauce.
Drizzle the sauce over the beef ribs and eat warm.

Beef Parmigiana Sliders

(Ready in about 15 minutes | Servings 2)

516 Calories; 20.7g Fat; 42g Carbs; 34.3g Protein; 5.1g Sugars

Ingredients

1/2 pound lean ground chuck
1 ounce bacon bits
2 tablespoons tomato paste
3 tablespoons shallots, chopped
1 garlic clove, minced
1/4 cup parmesan cheese, grated
1 teaspoon cayenne pepper
Salt and black pepper, to taste
4 pretzel rolls

Directions

Thoroughly combine the ground chuck, bacon bits, tomato paste, shallots, garlic, parmesan cheese, cayenne pepper, salt, black pepper. Shape the mixture into 4 equal patties.

Spritz your patties with a nonstick cooking spray. Air fry your burgers at 380 degrees F for about 11 minutes or to your desired degree of doneness.

Place your burgers on pretzel rolls and serve with favorite toppings. Enjoy!

Beef and Sausage Meatloaf with Peppers

(Ready in about 35 minutes | Servings 4)

415 Calories; 32.2g Fat; 4.4g Carbs; 25.3g Protein; 1.5g Sugars

Ingredients

1/2 pound beef sausage, crumbled
1/2 pound ground beef
1/4 cup pork rinds
2 tablespoons Parmesan, preferably freshly grated
1 shallot, finely chopped
2 garlic cloves, minced
Sea salt and ground black pepper, to taste
1 red bell pepper, finely chopped
1 serrano pepper, finely chopped

Directions

Start by preheating your Air Fryer to 390 degrees F.
Mix all ingredients in a bowl. Knead until everything is well incorporated.
Shape the mixture into a meatloaf and place in the baking pan that is previously greased with cooking oil.
Cook for 24 minutes in the preheated Air Fryer.
Let it stand on a cooling rack for 6 minutes before slicing and serving. Enjoy!

Birthday Party Cheeseburger Pizza

(Ready in about 20 minutes | Servings 4)

447 Calories; 16.1g Fat; 29.5g Carbs; 44.5g Protein; 2.7g Sugars

Ingredients

Nonstick cooking oil
1 pound ground beef
Kosher salt and ground black pepper, to taste
1/2 teaspoon oregano
1/2 teaspoon basil
1/4 teaspoon red pepper flakes
1/4 cup marinara sauce
2 spring onions, chopped

4 burger buns
1 cup mozzarella cheese, shredded

Directions

Start by preheating your Air Fryer to 370 degrees F. Spritz the Air Fryer basket with cooking oil.
Add the ground beef and cook for 10 minutes, crumbling with a spatula. Season with salt, black pepper, oregano, basil, and red peppers.
Spread the marinara pasta on each half of burger bun. Place the spring onions and ground meat mixture on the buns equally.
Set the temperature to 350 degrees F. Place the burger pizza in the Air Fryer basket. Top with mozzarella cheese.
Bake approximately 4 minutes or until cheese is bubbling. Top with another half of burger bun and serve. Bon appétit!

Kid-Friendly Mini Meatloaves

(Ready in about 30 minutes | Servings 4)

451 Calories; 27.6g Fat; 15.3g Carbs; 33.4g Protein; 3.7g Sugars

Ingredients

2 tablespoons bacon, chopped
1 small-sized onion, chopped
1 bell pepper, chopped
1 garlic clove, minced
1 pound ground beef
1/2 teaspoon dried basil
1/2 teaspoon dried mustard seeds
1/2 teaspoon dried marjoram
Salt and black pepper, to taste
1/2 cup panko crumbs
4 tablespoons tomato puree

Directions

Heat a nonstick skillet over medium-high heat; cook the bacon for 1 to 2 minutes; add the onion, bell pepper, and garlic and cook another 3 minutes or until fragrant.

Heat off. Stir in the ground beef, spices, and panko crumbs. Stir until well combined. Shape the mixture into four mini meatloaves.

Preheat your Air Fryer to 350 degrees F. Spritz the cooking basket with nonstick spray.

Place the mini meatloaves in the cooking basket and cook for 10 minutes; turn them over, top with the tomato puree and continue to cook for 10 minutes more. Bon appétit!

Steak Fingers with Lime Sauce

(Ready in about 20 minutes + marinating time | Servings 4)

471 Calories; 26.3g Fat; 13.9g Carbs; 42.5g Protein; 4.7g Sugars

Ingredients

1 ½ pounds sirloin steak
1/4 cup soy sauce
1/4 cup fresh lime juice
1 teaspoon garlic powder
1 teaspoon shallot powder
1 teaspoon celery seeds
1 teaspoon mustard seeds
Coarse sea salt and ground black pepper, to taste
1 teaspoon red pepper flakes
2 eggs, lightly whisked
1 cup breadcrumbs
1/4 cup parmesan cheese
1 teaspoon paprika

Directions

Place the steak, soy sauce, lime juice, garlic powder, shallot powder, celery seeds, mustard seeds, salt, black pepper, and red pepper in a large ceramic bowl; let it marinate for 3 hours.

Tenderize the cube steak by pounding with a mallet; cut into 1-inch strips. In a shallow bowl, whisk the eggs. In another bowl, mix the breadcrumbs, parmesan cheese, and paprika. Dip the beef pieces into the whisked eggs and coat on all sides. Now, dredge the beef pieces in the breadcrumb mixture. Cook at 400 degrees F for 14 minutes, flipping halfway through the cooking time. Meanwhile, make the sauce by heating the reserved marinade in a saucepan over medium heat; let it simmer until thoroughly warmed. Serve the steak fingers with the sauce on the side. Enjoy!

FIsh

Famous Tuna Niçoise Salad

(Ready in about 15 minutes | Servings 3)

315 Calories; 13g Fat; 11.5g Carbs; 37.3g Protein; 3.9g Sugars

Ingredients

1 pound tuna steak
Sea salt and ground black pepper, to taste
1/2 teaspoon red pepper flakes, crushed
1/4 teaspoon dried dill weed
1/2 teaspoon garlic paste
1 pound green beans, trimmed
2 handfuls baby spinach
2 handfuls iceberg lettuce, torn into pieces
1/2 red onion, sliced
1 cucumber, sliced
2 tablespoons lemon juice
1 tablespoon olive oil
1 teaspoon Dijon mustard
1 tablespoon balsamic vinegar
1 tablespoon roasted almonds, coarsely chopped
1 tablespoon fresh parsley, coarsely chopped

Directions

Pat the tuna steak dry; toss your tuna with salt, black pepper, red pepper, dill and garlic paste. Spritz your tuna with a nonstick cooking spray. Cook the tuna steak at 400 degrees F for 5 minutes; turn your tuna steak over and continue to cook for 4 to 5 minutes more.

Then, add the green beans to the cooking basket. Spritz green beans with a nonstick cooking spray. Cook at 400 degrees F for 5 minutes, shaking the basket once or twice. Cut your tuna into thin strips and transfer to a salad bowl; add in the green beans. Then, add in the baby spinach, iceberg lettuce, onion and cucumber and toss to combine. In a mixing bowl, whisk the lemon juice, olive oil, mustard and vinegar.

Dress the salad and garnish with roasted almonds and fresh parsley. Bon appétit!

Greek-Style Sea Bass

(Ready in about 15 minutes | Servings 2)

174 Calories; 4.8g Fat; 5g Carbs; 25.8g Protein; 2.6g Sugars

Ingredients

1/2 pound sea bass
1 garlic clove, halved
Sea salt and ground black pepper, to taste
1/2 teaspoon rigani (Greek oregano)
1/2 teaspoon dried dill weed
1/4 teaspoon ground bay leaf
1/4 teaspoon ground cumin 1/2 teaspoon shallot powder

Greek sauce:
1/2 Greek yogurt
1 teaspoon olive oil
1/2 teaspoon Tzatziki spice mix
1 teaspoon lime juice

Directions

Pat dry the sea bass with paper towels. Rub the fish with garlic halves.
Toss the fish with salt, black pepper, rigani, dill, ground bay leaf, ground cumin and shallot powder.
Cook the sea bass in your Air Fryer at 400 degrees F for 5 minutes; turn the filets over and cook on the other side for 5 to 6 minutes.
In the meantime, make the sauce by simply blending the remaining ingredients. Serve the warm fish dolloped with Greek-style sauce. Enjoy!

Halibut Steak with Zoodles and Lemon

(Ready in about 15 minutes | Servings 3)

341 Calories; 23.1g Fat; 8.2g Carbs; 26.3g Protein; 1.2g Sugars

Ingredients

1 pound halibut steak, cut into 3 pieces
1 garlic clove, halved
1 teaspoon avocado oil
Sea salt and black pepper, to taste
1 pound zucchini, julienned
1/2 teaspoon onion powder
1/2 teaspoon granulated garlic
1 tablespoon fresh parsley, minced
1 teaspoon sage, minced
1 lemon, sliced

Directions

Rub the halibut steaks with garlic and toss with avocado oil, salt and black pepper; then, transfer the halibut steaks to the Air Fryer cooking basket.
Cook the halibut steak at 400 degrees F for 5 minutes. Turn the halibut steak over and continue to cook an additional 5 minutes or until it flakes easily when tested with a fork.
Meanwhile, spritz a wok with a nonstick spray; heat the wok over medium-high heat.
Once hot, stir fry the zucchini noodles along with the onion powder and granulated garlic; cook for 2 to 3 minutes or until just tender.
Top your zoodles with the parsley and sage and stir to combine.
Serve the hot zoodles with the halibut steaks and lemon slices. Bon appétit!

Roasted Mediterranean Snapper Fillets

(Ready in about 20 minutes + marinating time | Servings 3)

271 Calories; 4.6g Fat; 21.8g Carbs; 34.9g Protein; 4.9g Sugars

Ingredients

Marinade:
1 tablespoon black olives, chopped
1/4 cup dry white wine
2 tablespoons fresh lemon juice
1/2 teaspoon dried oregano
1/2 teaspoon dried basil
1 tablespoon parsley leaves, chopped
1 tomato, pureed
Roasted Snapper:
1 pound snapper fillets
1/2 cup cassava flour
Salt and white pepper, to taste

Directions

Add all ingredients for the marinade to a large ceramic bowl. Add the snapper fillets and let them marinate for 1 hour in your refrigerator.

Place the cassava flour on a tray; now, coat the snapper fillets with the cassava flour. Season with salt and pepper.

Cook the snapper fillets in the preheated Air Fryer at 395 degrees F for 10 minutes, basting with the marinade and flipping them halfway through the cooking time. Bon appétit!

Quick-Fix Seafood Breakfast

(Ready in about 30 minutes | Servings 2)

414 Calories; 23.4g Fat; 11.6g Carbs; 38.8g Protein; 7.2g Sugars

Ingredients

1 tablespoon olive oil
2 garlic cloves, minced
1 small yellow onion, chopped
1/4 pound tilapia pieces
1/4 pound rockfish pieces
1/2 teaspoon dried basil
Salt and white pepper, to taste
4 eggs, lightly beaten
1 tablespoon dry sherry
4 tablespoons cheese, shredded

Directions

Start by preheating your Air Fryer to 350 degrees F; add the olive oil to a baking pan. Once hot, cook the garlic and onion for 2 minutes or until fragrant.

Add the fish, basil, salt, and pepper. In a mixing dish, thoroughly combine the eggs with sherry and cheese. Pour the mixture into the baking pan.

Cook at 360 degrees F approximately 20 minutes. Bon appétit!

Shrimp Scampi Dip with Cheese

(Ready in about 25 minutes | Servings 8)

135 Calories; 9.7g Fat; 3.3g Carbs; 8.7g Protein; 1g Sugars

Ingredients

2 teaspoons butter, melted
8 ounces shrimp, peeled and deveined
2 garlic cloves, minced
1/4 cup chicken stock
2 tablespoons fresh lemon juice
Salt and ground black pepper, to taste
1/2 teaspoon red pepper flakes
4 ounces cream cheese, at room temperature
1/2 cup sour cream
4 tablespoons mayonnaise
1/4 cup mozzarella cheese, shredded

Directions

Start by preheating the Air Fryer to 395 degrees F. Grease the sides and bottom of a baking dish with the melted butter.

Place the shrimp, garlic, chicken stock, lemon juice, salt, black pepper, and red pepper flakes in the baking dish.

Transfer the baking dish to the cooking basket and bake for 10 minutes. Add the mixture to your food processor; pulse until the coarsely is chopped.

Add the cream cheese, sour cream, and mayonnaise. Top with the mozzarella cheese and bake in the preheated Air Fryer at 360 degrees F for 6 to 7 minutes or until the cheese is bubbling.

Serve immediately with breadsticks if desired. Bon appétit!

Vegetable and Side Dishes

Hot Mexican Corn on the Cob

(Ready in about 10 minutes | Servings 2)

239 Calories; 9.8g Fat; 30.2g Carbs; 11.5g Protein; 5.4g Sugars

Ingredients

1 ears corn
1/2 cup Mexican crema
1 teaspoon chili powder
2 tablespoons cilantro leaves, minced
1 lime, freshly squeezed

Directions

Husk the corn and pull off the silky threads.
In a shallow dish, mix the Mexican crema, chili powder, cilantro and lime juice.
Cook the corn in the preheated Air Fryer at 390 degrees F for about 4 minutes.
Rub each ear of corn with the Mexican crema mixture and continue to cook for 2 minutes more. Salt to taste and serve immediately.

Mexican-Style Roasted Zucchini

(Ready in about 15 minutes | Servings 3)

137 Calories; 8.8g Fat; 6.9g Carbs; 9.9g Protein; 0.9g Sugars

Ingredients

1 pound zucchini, sliced into thick rounds
1 teaspoon chili oil
1/2 teaspoon red pepper flakes, crushed
1/2 teaspoon garlic powder
1/8 teaspoon cayenne pepper
1 teaspoon Mexican oregano
Kosher salt and black pepper, to taste
1/2 cup Cotija cheese, crumbled
1 tablespoon fresh cilantro, roughly chopped

Directions

Toss your zucchini with the chili oil, red pepper flakes, garlic powder, cayenne pepper, Mexican oregano, salt and black pepper. Transfer your zucchini to the Air Fryer cooking basket.
Cook your zucchini at 400 degrees F for 7 minutes. Turn over the slices of zucchini and top them with crumbled cheese.
Continue to cook for 5 minutes more. Garnish with cilantro and serve.

Favorite Winter Bliss Bowl

(Ready in about 25 minutes | Servings 3)

166 Calories; 3.9g Fat; 32g Carbs; 4.5g Protein; 3.3g Sugars

Ingredients

1 pound cauliflower florets
9 ounces frozen crab cakes
1 teaspoon olive oil
Sea salt and freshly ground black pepper, to taste
1 cup quinoa
1 cup iceberg lettuce
1 cup baby spinach
1 red bell pepper, deseeded and sliced
2 tablespoons fresh lemon juice
1 tablespoon extra-virgin olive oil
1 teaspoon yellow mustard
2 tablespoons cilantro leaves, chopped

Directions

Brush the cauliflower and crab cakes with olive oil; season them with salt and black pepper and transfer them to the cooking basket. Cook the cauliflower at 400 degrees F for about 12 minutes total, shaking the basket halfway through the cooking time. Then, cook the crab cakes at 400 degrees F for about 12 minutes total, flipping them halfway through the cooking time. In the meantime, rinse your quinoa, drain it and transfer to a soup pot with 2 cups of lightly salted water; bring to a boil. Turn heat to a simmer and continue to cook, covered, for about 20 minutes; fluff with a fork and transfer to a serving bowl. Add the cauliflower and crab cakes to the bowl. Add your greens and bell pepper to the bowl. In a small mixing dish, whisk the lemon juice, extra-virgin olive oil and yellow mustard. Drizzle the dressing over all ingredients, garnish with fresh cilantro and serve immediately. Bon appétit!

Classic Onion Rings

(Ready in about 30 minutes | Servings 2)

440 Calories; 12.7g Fat; 60g Carbs; 19.2g Protein; 5.6g Sugars

Ingredients

1 medium-sized onion, slice into rings
1 cup all-purpose flour
1 teaspoon baking powder
Coarse sea salt and ground black pepper, to your liking
1/2 cup yogurt
2 eggs, beaten
3/4 cup bread crumbs
1 teaspoon onion powder
1 teaspoon garlic powder
1/2 teaspoon celery seeds

Directions

Place the onion rings in the bowl with cold water; let them soak approximately 20 minutes; drain the onion rings and pat dry using a pepper towel.
In a shallow bowl, mix the flour, baking powder, salt, and black pepper. Add the yogurt and eggs and mix well to combine.
In another shallow bowl, mix the bread crumbs, onion powder, garlic powder, and celery seeds. Dip the onion rings in the flour/egg mixture; then, dredge in the breadcrumb mixture.
Spritz the Air Fryer basket with cooking spray; arrange the breaded onion rings in the basket.
Cook in the preheated Air Fryer at 400 degrees F for 4 to 5 minutes, turning them over halfway through the cooking time. Bon appétit!

Cauliflower and Goat Cheese Croquettes

(Ready in about 30 minutes | Servings 2)

297 Calories; 21.7g Fat; 11.7g Carbs; 15.3g Protein; 2.6g Sugars

Ingredients

1/2 pound cauliflower florets
2 garlic cloves, minced
1 cup goat cheese, shredded
Sea salt and ground black pepper, to taste
1/2 teaspoon shallot powder
1/4 teaspoon cumin powder
1 cup sour cream
1 teaspoon Dijon mustard

Directions

Place the cauliflower florets in a saucepan of water; bring to the boil; reduce the heat and cook for 10 minutes or until tender.
Mash the cauliflower using your blender; add the garlic, cheese, and spices; mix to combine well.
Form the cauliflower mixture into croquettes shapes.
Cook in the preheated Air Fryer at 375 degrees F for 16 minutes, shaking halfway through the cooking time. Serve with the sour cream and mustard. Bon appétit!

Tater Tot Vegetable Casserole

(Ready in about 40 minutes | Servings 6)

493 Calories; 26.1g Fat; 49.6g Carbs; 17.1g Protein; 5.7g Sugars

Ingredients

1 tablespoon olive oil
1 shallot, sliced
2 cloves garlic, minced
1 red bell pepper, seeded and sliced
1 yellow bell pepper, seeded and sliced
1 ½ cups kale
1 (28-ounce) bag frozen tater tots
6 eggs
1 cup milk
Sea salt and ground black pepper, to your liking
1 cup Swiss cheese, shredded
4 tablespoons seasoned breadcrumbs

Directions

Heat the olive oil in a saucepan over medium-high heat. Sauté the shallot, garlic, and peppers for 2 to 3 minutes. Add the kale and cook until wilted.

Arrange the tater tots evenly over the bottom of a lightly greased casserole dish. Spread the sautéed mixture over the top.

In a mixing bowl, thoroughly combine the eggs, milk, salt, pepper, and shredded cheese. Pour the mixture into the casserole dish.

Lastly, top with the seasoned breadcrumbs. Bake at 330 degrees F for 30 minutes or until top is golden brown. Bon appétit!

Snacks & Appetizers

Beer-Battered Vidalia Onion Rings

(Ready in about 15 minutes | Servings 2)

269 Calories; 4.1g Fat; 48.1g Carbs; 7.9g Protein; 7.7g Sugars

Ingredients

1/2 cup all-purpose flour
1/2 teaspoon baking powder
1/4 teaspoon cayenne pepper
1/4 teaspoon dried oregano
Kosher salt and ground black pepper, to taste
1 large egg, beaten
1/4 cup beer
1 cup crushed tortilla chips
1/2 pound Vidalia onions, cut into rings

Directions

In a mixing bowl, thoroughly combine the flour, baking powder, cayenne pepper, oregano, salt, black pepper, egg and beer; mix to combine well.

In another shallow bowl, place the crushed tortilla chips.

Dip the Vidalia rings in the beer mixture; then, coat the rings with the crushed tortilla chips, pressing to adhere.

Transfer the onion rings to the Air Fryer cooking basket and spritz them with a nonstick spray.

Cook the onion rings at 380 degrees F for about 8 minutes, shaking the basket halfway through the cooking time to ensure even browning. Bon appétit!

Pepper and Bacon Mini Skewers

(Ready in about 10 minutes | Servings 4)

198 Calories; 11.5g Fat; 17.1g Carbs; 5.1g Protein; 11.1g Sugars

Ingredients

4 ounces bacon, diced
2 bell peppers, sliced
1/4 cup barbecue sauce
1 teaspoon Ranch seasoning blend
1/2 cup tomato sauce
1 teaspoon jalapeno, minced

Directions

Assemble the skewers alternating bacon and bell pepper. Toss them with barbecue sauce and Ranch seasoning blend.
Cook the mini skewers in the preheated Air Fryer at 400 degrees F for 6 minutes.
Mix the tomato sauce and minced jalapeno. Bon appétit!

Hot Paprika Bacon Deviled Eggs

(Ready in about 15 minutes | Servings 4)

178 Calories; 14.3g Fat; 3.6g Carbs; 8.6g Protein; 2.3g Sugars

Ingredients

4 eggs
2 ounces bacon bits
2 tablespoons mayonnaise
2 tablespoons cream cheese 1 teaspoon hot sauce
1/2 teaspoon garlic, minced
1 tablespoon pickle relish
1/2 teaspoon hot paprika
Salt and ground black pepper, to taste

Directions

Place the wire rack in the Air Fryer basket and lower the eggs onto the rack.
Cook the eggs at 260 degrees F for 15 minutes.
Transfer the eggs to an ice-cold water bath to stop cooking. Peel the eggs under cold running water; slice them into halves, separating the whites and yolks.
Mash the egg yolks; add in the remaining ingredients and stir to combine; spoon the yolk mixture into the egg whites.
Bon appétit!

Quick and Easy Popcorn

(Ready in about 20 minutes | Servings 4)

41 Calories; 1.9g Fat; 4.9g Carbs; 1g Protein; 0.6g Sugars

Ingredients

2 tablespoons dried corn kernels
1 teaspoon safflower oil
Kosher salt, to taste
1 teaspoon red pepper flakes, crushed

Directions

Add the dried corn kernels to the Air Fryer basket; brush with safflower oil.

Cook at 395 degrees F for 15 minutes, shaking the basket every 5 minutes.

Sprinkle with salt and red pepper flakes. Bon appétit!

Hot Cheesy Mushrooms Bites

(Ready in about 10 minutes | Servings 3)

203 Calories; 14.3g Fat; 7.4g Carbs; 13.3g Protein; 1.5g Sugars

Ingredients

1 teaspoon butter, melted
1 teaspoon fresh garlic, finely minced
4 ounces cheddar cheese, grated
4 tablespoons tortilla chips, crushed
1 tablespoon fresh coriander, chopped
1/2 teaspoon hot sauce
12 button mushrooms, stalks removed and chopped
Sea salt and ground black pepper, to taste

Directions

In a mixing bowl, thoroughly combine the butter, garlic, cheddar cheese, tortilla chips, coriander, hot sauce and chopped mushrooms. Divide the filling among mushroom caps and transfer them to the air Fryer cooking basket; season them with salt and black pepper.
Cook your mushrooms in the preheated Air Fryer at 400 degrees F for 5 minutes.
Transfer the warm mushrooms to a serving platter and serve at room temperature. Bon appétit!

Sea Scallops and Bacon Skewers

(Ready in about 50 minutes | Servings 6)

138 Calories; 3.6g Fat; 8.3g Carbs; 17.6g Protein; 5.5g Sugars

Ingredients

1/2 pound sea scallops
1/2 cup coconut milk
6 ounces orange juice
1 tablespoon vermouth
Sea salt and ground black pepper, to taste
1/2 pound bacon, diced
1 shallot, diced
1 teaspoon garlic powder
1 teaspoon paprika

Directions

In a ceramic bowl, place the sea scallops, coconut milk, orange juice, vermouth, salt, and black pepper; let it marinate for 30 minutes.
Assemble the skewers alternating the scallops, bacon, and shallots.
Sprinkle garlic powder and paprika all over the skewers.
Bake in the preheated air Fryer at 400 degrees F for 6 minutes. Serve warm and enjoy!

Rice and Grain

Chocolate Chip Bread Pudding Squares

(Ready in about 20 minutes | Servings 3)

339 Calories; 18.4g Fat; 34.6g Carbs; 6.5g Protein; 21.2g Sugars

Ingredients

3 thick slices bread, cut into cubes
1 egg
1 cup heavy cream
1 tablespoon agave nectar
1/4 teaspoon ground cinnamon
1/4 teaspoon ground cloves
2 tablespoons chocolate chips
2 tablespoons icing sugar

Directions

Add the bread chunks to a lightly oiled baking dish.

In a mixing dish, whisk the egg, heavy cream, agave nectar, cinnamon and cloves. Pour the custard over the bread chunks and press to soak well.

Fold in the chocolate chips.

Cook in the preheated Air Fryer at 370 degrees F for about 13 minutes.

Place the bread pudding in the refrigerator until it is chilled completely; cut into 1 ½-inch squares.

Bake the squares at 330 degrees F for 2 minutes until golden on the top. Dust with icing sugar and serve. Bon appétit!

Italian-Style Fried Polenta Slices

(Ready in about 35 minutes | Servings 3)

451 Calories; 4.4g Fat; 91g Carbs; 11.2g Protein; 0g Sugars

Ingredients

9 ounces pre-cooked polenta roll
1 teaspoon sesame oil
2 ounces prosciutto, chopped
1 teaspoon Italian seasoning blend

Directions

Cut the pre-cooked polenta roll into nine equal slices. Brush them with sesame oil on all sides. Then, transfer the polenta slices to the lightly oiled Air Fryer cooking basket.
Cook the polenta slices at 395 degrees F for about 30 minutes; then, top them with chopped prosciutto and Italian seasoning blend. Continue to cook for another 5 minutes until cooked through. Serve with marinara sauce, if desired. Bon appétit!

Beef Taquito Casserole

(Ready in about 20 minutes | Servings 4)

364 Calories; 19g Fat; 32.8g Carbs; 16g Protein; 2.8g Sugars

Ingredients

1/2 (15-ounce) can black beans, drained and rinsed well
1 tablespoon taco seasoning mix
4 ounces mild enchilada sauce
1 cup Mexican cheese blend, shredded
1/2 (20-ounce) box frozen taquitos (chicken and cheese in tortillas)
2 tablespoons fresh chives, roughly chopped

Directions

Start by preheating your Air Fryer to 350 degrees F. Spritz the baking pan with cooking spray.
Mix the beans, taco seasoning mix, enchilada sauce and 1/2 cups of shredded cheese in the baking dish.
Top the mixture with taquitos. Bake for 15 minutes. Top with the remaining 1/2 cup of shredded cheese and bake for a further 15 minutes.
Serve garnished with chopped chives. Enjoy!

Ciabatta Bread Pudding with Walnuts

(Ready in about 45 minutes | Servings 4)

454 Calories; 18.2g Fat; 56.7g Carbs; 18.3g Protein; 25.1g Sugars

Ingredients

4 cups ciabatta bread cubes
2 eggs, slightly beaten
1 cup milk
2 tablespoons butter
4 tablespoons honey
1 teaspoon vanilla extract
1/2 teaspoon ground cloves
1/2 teaspoon ground cinnamon
A pinch of salt
A pinch of grated nutmeg
1/3 cup walnuts, chopped

Directions

Place the ciabatta bread cubes in a lightly greased baking dish. In a mixing bowl, thoroughly combine the eggs, milk, butter, honey, vanilla, ground cloves, cinnamon, salt, and nutmeg.

Pour the custard over the bread cubes. Scatter the chopped walnuts over the top of your bread pudding.

Let stand for 30 minutes, occasionally pressing with a wide spatula to submerge.

Cook in the preheated Air Fryer at 370 degrees F degrees for 7 minutes; check to ensure even cooking and cook an additional 5 to 6 minutes. Bon appétit!

Paella-Style Spanish Rice

(Ready in about 35 minutes | Servings 2)

546 Calories; 12.4g Fat; 90.7g Carbs; 17.6g Protein; 4.5g Sugars

Ingredients

2 cups water
1 cup white rice, rinsed and drained
1 cube vegetable stock
1 chorizo, sliced

2 cups brown mushrooms, cleaned and sliced

2 cloves garlic, finely chopped
1/2 teaspoon fresh ginger, ground
1 long red chili, minced
1/4 cup dry white wine
1/2 cup tomato sauce
1 teaspoon smoked paprika
Kosher salt and ground black pepper, to taste
1 cup green beans

Directions

In a medium saucepan, bring the water to a boil. Add the rice and vegetable stock cube. Stir and reduce the heat. Cover and let it simmer for 20 minutes.

Then, place the chorizo, mushrooms, garlic, ginger, and red chili in the baking pan. Cook at 380 degrees F for 6 minutes, stirring periodically.

Add the prepared rice to the casserole dish. Add the remaining ingredients and gently stir to combine.

Cook for 6 minutes, checking periodically to ensure even cooking.

Serve in individual bowls and enjoy!

Air Grilled Cheese Roll-Ups

(Ready in about 10 minutes | Servings 3)

395 Calories; 26.4g Fat; 21.1g Carbs; 16.9g Protein; 2.5g Sugars

Ingredients

6 slices bread
2 tablespoons butter
6 slices Colby cheese
A pinch of ground black pepper

Directions

Flatten the bread slices to 1/4-inch thickness using a rolling pin.
Spread the melted butter on top of each slice of bread.
Place a cheese slice on top of each slice of bread; sprinkle with black pepper and roll them up tightly.
Bake the cheese roll-ups at 390 degrees F for about 8 minutes. Bon appétit!

Vegan

Decadent Carrot Salad with Sultanas

(Ready in about 20 minutes | Servings 3)

208 Calories; 8.3g Fat; 32.1g Carbs; 4.8g Protein; 19.4g Sugars

Ingredients

1 pound carrots, cut into 1/2-inch slices

1/4 teaspoon dried dill
1/2 teaspoon dried parsley flakes
2 tablespoons maple syrup
2 tablespoons Sultanas
1/2 cup orange juice
1 tablespoon champagne vinegar
6 ounces baby spinach
1/4 cup pine nuts, roughly chopped

Directions

Toss your carrots with dried dill and dried parsley flakes; brush them with a nonstick cooking spray.
Cook your carrots in the preheated Air Fryer at 380 degrees F for about 15 minutes, shaking the basket halfway through the cooking time.
Meanwhile, add the maple syrup, Sultanas, orange juice and champagne vinegar to a saucepan; let it simmer over a moderate heat until the sauce has thickened.
Spoon the sauce over the roasted carrots and stir in the baby spinach. Top with chopped pine nuts and serve at room temperature. Bon appétit!

Authentic Platanos Maduros

(Ready in about 15 minutes | Servings 2)

129 Calories; 2.5g Fat; 28.2g Carbs; 1.1g Protein; 13.4g Sugars

Ingredients

1 very ripe, sweet plantain
1 teaspoon Caribbean Sorrel Rum Spice Mix
1 teaspoon coconut oil, melted

Directions

Cut your plantain into slices.
Toss your plantain with Caribbean Sorrel Rum Spice Mix and coconut oil.
Cook your plantain in the preheated Air Fryer at 400 degrees F for 10 minutes, shaking the cooking basket halfway through the cooking time.
Serve immediately and enjoy!

Spicy Sesame Cauliflower Steaks

(Ready in about 25 minutes | Servings 2)

247 Calories; 0.8g Fat; 54.4g Carbs; 6.6g Protein; 10.1g Sugars

Ingredients

1/2 pound cauliflower, cut into 2 slabs
1/2 cup plain flour
1/4 cup cornstarch
1/2 cup ale
1/2 teaspoon hot sauce
1/4 teaspoon onion powder
1/2 teaspoon garlic powder
1/2 teaspoon smoked paprika
1 tablespoon sesame seeds

Kosher salt and ground black pepper, to taste
1/4 cup buffalo sauce

Directions

Parboil the cauliflower in the pot with a lightly salted water for about 15 minutes.
In a mixing bowl, combine the remaining ingredients, except for the buffalo sauce, until everything is well incorporated. Then, dip the cauliflower steaks into the batter.
Cook the cauliflower steaks at 400 degrees F for 10 minutes, flipping them over halfway through the cooking time to promote even cooking.
Serve the warm cauliflower steaks with buffalo sauce and enjoy!

Traditional Indian Pakora

(Ready in about 35 minutes | Servings 2)

175 Calories; 4.4g Fat; 24.6g Carbs; 9.5g Protein; 3.9g Sugars

Ingredients

1 large zucchini, grated

1/2 cup besan flour
1/2 teaspoon baking powder
2 scallion stalks, chopped
1/2 teaspoon paprika
1/4 teaspoon curry powder
14 teaspoon ginger-garlic paste
Sea salt and ground black pepper, to taste
1 teaspoon olive oil

Directions

Sprinkle the salt over the grated zucchini and leave it for 20 minutes. Then, squeeze the zucchini and drain off the excess liquid.
Mix the grated zucchini with the flour, baking powder, scallions, paprika, curry powder and ginger-garlic paste. Salt and pepper to taste.
Shape the mixture into patties and transfer them to the Air Fryer cooking basket. Brush the zucchini patties with 1 teaspoon of olive oil.
Cook the pakora at 380 degrees F for about 12 minutes, flipping them halfway through the cooking time.
Serve on dinner rolls and enjoy!

Barbecue Tofu with Green Beans

(Ready in about 1 hour | Servings 3)

316 Calories; 19.8g Fat; 20.8g Carbs; 20.1g Protein; 8.1g Sugars

Ingredients

12 ounces super firm tofu, pressed and cubed
1/4 cup ketchup
1 tablespoon white vinegar
1 tablespoon coconut sugar
1 tablespoon mustard
1/4 teaspoon ground black pepper
1/2 teaspoon sea salt
1/4 teaspoon smoked paprika
1/2 teaspoon freshly grated ginger
2 cloves garlic, minced
2 tablespoons olive oil
1 pound green beans

Directions

Toss the tofu with the ketchup, white vinegar, coconut sugar, mustard, black pepper, sea salt, paprika, ginger, garlic, and olive oil. Let it marinate for 30 minutes.
Cook at 360 degrees F for 10 minutes; turn them over and cook for 12 minutes more. Reserve.
Place the green beans in the lightly greased Air Fryer basket. Roast at 400 degrees F for 5 minutes. Bon appétit!

Polish Placki Ziemniaczan

(Ready in about 10 minutes | Servings 2)

262 Calories; 3.7g Fat; 50.1g Carbs; 6.4g Protein; 10.3g Sugars

Ingredients

1/2 pound potatoes, peeled and finely grated
1/2 small white onion, finely chopped
1/4 cup all-purpose flour
1/2 teaspoon turmeric powder
2 tablespoons breadcrumbs
Kosher salt and freshly ground black pepper, to taste
2 tablespoons granulated sugar
2 ounces sour cream

Directions

Place the grated potatoes in a triple layer of cheesecloth; now, twist and squeeze the potatoes until no more liquid comes out of them.
Place the potatoes in a mixing bowl; stir in the onion, flour, turmeric powder, breadcrumbs, salt and black pepper.
Cook them at 380 degrees for about 10 minutes, turning over after 5 minutes. Serve with granulated sugar and sour cream. Enjoy!

Dessert

Crunchy French Toast Sticks

(Ready in about 10 minutes | Servings 3)

188 Calories; 8.3g Fat; 21.9g Carbs; 6.2g Protein; 6.1g Sugars

Ingredients

1 egg
1/4 cup double cream
1/4 cup milk
1 tablespoon brown sugar
1/4 teaspoon ground cloves
1/4 teaspoon ground cinnamon
1/4 vanilla paste
3 thick slices of brioche bread, cut into thirds
1 cup crispy rice cereal

Directions

Thoroughly combine the egg, cream, milk, sugar, ground cloves, cinnamon and vanilla.
Dip each piece of bread into the cream mixture and then, press gently into the cereal, pressing to coat all sides.
Arrange the pieces of bread in the Air Fryer cooking basket and cook them at 380 degrees F for 2 minutes; flip and cook on the other side for 2 to 3 minutes longer.
Bon appétit!

TOAST

Old-Fashioned Baked Pears

(Ready in about 10 minutes | Servings 2)

445 Calories; 14g Fat; 89g Carbs; 9g Protein; 49.1g Sugars

Ingredients

2 large pears, halved and cored
1 teaspoon lemon juice

2 teaspoons coconut oil

1/2 cup rolled oats
1/4 cup walnuts, chopped
1/4 cup brown sugar
1 teaspoon apple pie spice mix

Directions

Drizzle the pear halves with lemon juice and coconut oil. In a mixing bowl, thoroughly combine the rolled oats, walnuts, brown sugar and apple pie spice mix.
Cook in the preheated Air Fryer at 360 degrees for 8 minutes, checking them halfway through the cooking time.
Dust with powdered sugar if desired. Bon appétit!

Chocolate Puff Pastry Sticks

(Ready in about 15 minutes | Servings 3)

407 Calories; 21.2g Fat; 46.1g Carbs; 6.9g Protein; 5.5g Sugars

Ingredients

8 ounces frozen puff pastry, thawed, cut into strips
1/2 stick butter, melted
1/2 teaspoon ground cinnamon
1/2 cup chocolate hazelnut spread

Directions

Brush the strips of the puff pastry with melted butter.
Arrange the strips in the Air Fryer cooking basket and bake them at 380 degrees F for 2 minutes; flip and cook on the other side for 2 to 3 minutes longer.
Top the pastry sticks with cinnamon and chocolate hazelnut spread. Bon appétit!

Nana's Famous Apple Fritters

(Ready in about 20 minutes | Servings 4)

280 Calories; 5.7g Fat; 51.1g Carbs; 7.4g Protein; 30.8g Sugars

Ingredients

2/3 cup all-purpose flour
1 tablespoons granulated sugar
A pinch of sea salt
A pinch of freshly grated nutmeg
1 teaspoon baking powder
2 eggs, whisked
1/4 cup milk
2 apples, peeled, cored and diced
1/2 cup powdered sugar

Directions

Mix the flour, sugar, salt, nutmeg and baking powder.
In a separate bowl whisk the eggs with the milk; add this wet mixture into the dry ingredients; mix to combine well.
Add the apple pieces and mix again.
Cook in the preheated Air Fryer at 370 degrees for 3 minutes, flipping them halfway through the cooking time. Repeat with the remaining batter.
Dust with powdered sugar and serve at room temperature. Bon appétit!

The Ultimate Berry Crumble

(Ready in about 40 minutes | Servings 6)

272 Calories; 8.3g Fat; 49.5g Carbs; 3.3g Protein; 31g Sugars

Ingredients

18 ounces cherries
1/2 cup granulated sugar
2 tablespoons cornmeal
1/4 teaspoon ground star anise
1/2 teaspoon ground cinnamon
2/3 cup all-purpose flour
1 cup demerara sugar
1/2 teaspoon baking powder
1/3 cup rolled oats
1/2 stick butter, cut into small pieces

Directions

Toss the cherries with the granulated sugar, cornmeal, star anise, and cinnamon. Divide between six custard cups coated with cooking spray.
In a mixing dish, thoroughly combine the remaining ingredients. Sprinkle over the berry mixture.
Bake in the preheated Air Fryer at 330 degrees F for 35 minutes. Bon appétit!

Old-Fashioned Baked Pears

(Ready in about 10 minutes | Servings 2)

445 Calories; 14g Fat; 89g Carbs; 9g Protein; 49.1g Sugars

Ingredients

2 large pears, halved and cored
1 teaspoon lemon juice
1 teaspoons coconut oil
1/2 cup rolled oats
1/4 cup walnuts, chopped
1/4 cup brown sugar
1 teaspoon apple pie spice mix

Directions

Drizzle the pear halves with lemon juice and coconut oil. In a mixing bowl, thoroughly combine the rolled oats, walnuts, brown sugar and apple pie spice mix.
Cook in the preheated Air Fryer at 360 degrees for 8 minutes, checking them halfway through the cooking time.
Dust with powdered sugar if desired. Bon appétit!

Other Air Fryer

Chicken Burgers

509 Calories; 9.8g Fat; 34g Carbs; 39.2g Protein; 7.3g Sugars

Ingredients

1 ¼ pounds chicken white meat, ground 1/2 white onion, finely chopped
1 teaspoon fresh garlic, finely chopped Sea salt and ground black pepper, to taste 1 teaspoon paprika
1/2 cup cornmeal
1 ½ cups breadcrumbs 4 burger buns
4 lettuce leaves
2 small pickles, sliced 2 tablespoons ketchup
1 teaspoon yellow mustard

Directions

Thoroughly combine the chicken, onion, garlic, salt and black pepper in a mixing dish. Form the mixture into 4 equal patties.
In a shallow bowl, mix paprika with cornmeal and breadcrumbs. Dip each patty in this mixture, pressing to coat well on both sides.
Spritz a cooking basket with a nonstick cooking spray. Air fry the burgers at 370 degrees F for about 11 minutes or to your desired degree of doneness.
Place your burgers on burger buns and serve with toppings.

Chicken Nuggets and Turnip Chips

361 Calories; 19.1g Fat; 9.6g Carbs; 35g Protein; 1.1g Sugars

Ingredients

1 egg
1/2 teaspoon cayenne pepper 1/3 cup panko crumbs
1/4 teaspoon Romano cheese, grated 2 teaspoons canola oil
1 pound chicken breast, cut into slices
1 medium-sized turnip, trimmed and sliced 1/2 teaspoon garlic powder
Sea salt and ground black pepper, to taste

Directions

Beat the egg with the cayenne pepper until frothy. In another shallow bowl, mix the panko crumbs with the cheese until well combined.
Dip the chicken slices into the egg mixture; then, coat the chicken slices on all sides with the the panko mixture. Brush with 1 teaspoon of canola oil. Season with salt and pepper to taste.
Cook in the preheated Air Fryer at 380 degrees F for 12 minutes, shaking the basket halfway through the cooking time; an instant-read thermometer should read 165 degrees F. Reserve, keeping them warm.
Drizzle the turnip slices with the remaining teaspoon of canola oil. Season with garlic powder, salt and pepper to taste.
Cook the turnips slices at 370 degrees F for about 20 minutes. Serve with the warm chicken nuggets.

Fried pork ribs

379 Calories; 12g Fat; 19.1g Carbs; 45.5g Protein; 2.3g Sugars

Ingredients

1 egg
1/4 cup cornmeal
1/4 cup crackers, crushed 1/2 teaspoon garlic powder 1/2 teaspoon cayenne pepper
Salt and black pepper, to taste
2 boneless pork loin chops, about 1-inch thick, 6 ounces each

Directions

In a shallow mixing bowl, whisk the egg until pale and frothy.
In another bowl, mix the cornmeal, crushed crackers, garlic powder, cayenne pepper, salt and black pepper.
Dip each pork loin chop in the beaten egg. Then, roll them over the cornmeal mixture.
Spritz the bottom of the cooking basket with cooking oil. Add the breaded pork cutlets and cook at 395 degrees F for 6 minutes.
Flip and cook for 6 minutes on the other side. Serve warm.

Chuck Roast in sweet sauce

325 Calories; 16.8g Fat; 13.7g Carbs; 31.9g Protein; 12.8g Sugars

Ingredients

1 pound chuck roast
Sea salt and ground black pepper, to taste 2 tablespoons butter, softened
1 tablespoon coriander, chopped
1 tablespoon fresh scallions, chopped 1 teaspoon soy sauce
1 tablespoon fish sauce 2 tablespoons honey

Directions

Season the chuck roast with salt and pepper; spritz a nonstick cooking oil all over the beef.
Air fry at 400 degrees F for 30 to 35 minutes, flipping the chuck roast halfway through the cooking time.
While the roast is cooking, heat the other ingredients in a sauté pan over medium-high heat. Bring to a boil and reduce the heat; let it simmer, partially covered, until the sauce has thickened and reduced.
Slice the chuck roast into thick cuts and serve garnished with sweet 'n' sticky sauce.

Simple burgers

433 Calories; 17.4g Fat; 40g Carbs; 39.2g Protein; 6.4g Sugars

Ingredients

3/4 pound lean ground chuck
Kosher salt and ground black pepper, to taste 3 tablespoons onion, minced
1 teaspoon garlic, minced 1 teaspoon soy sauce
1/2 teaspoon smoked paprika 1/4 teaspoon ground cumin 1/2 teaspoon cayenne pepper 1/2 teaspoon mustard seeds 2 burger buns

Directions

Thoroughly combine the ground chuck, salt, black pepper, onion, garlic and soy sauce in a mixing dish.
Season with smoked paprika, ground cumin, cayenne pepper and mustard seeds. Mix to combine well.
Shape the mixture into 2 equal patties.
Spritz your patties with a nonstick cooking spray. Air fry your burgers at 380 degrees F for about 11 minutes or to your desired degree of doneness.
Place your burgers on burger buns and serve with favorite toppings. Devour!

Cod fillets

218 Calories; 12.5g Fat; 3.5g Carbs; 22g Protein; 1.9g Sugars

Ingredients

2 cod fish fillets
1 teaspoon butter, melted
1 teaspoon Old Bay seasoning 1 egg, beaten
2 tablespoons coconut milk, unsweetened 1/3 cup coconut flour, unsweetened

Directions

Place the cod fish fillets, butter and Old Bay seasoning in a Ziplock bag; shake until the fish is well coated on all sides.
In a shallow bowl, whisk the egg and coconut milk until frothy.
In another bowl, place the coconut flour. Dip the fish fillets in the egg mixture, then, coat them with coconut flour, pressing to adhere.
Cook the fish at 390 degrees F for 6 minutes; flip them over and cook an additional 6 minutes until your fish flakes easily when tested with a fork.

Mediterranean broccoli

199 Calories; 15.6g Fat; 11.3g Carbs; 4.6g Protein; 2.8g Sugars

Ingredients

1 pound broccoli florets 1 teaspoon butter, melted Sea salt, to taste
1 teaspoon mixed peppercorns, crushed 1/4 cup mayonnaise
1 tablespoon fresh lemon juice 1 teaspoon deli mustard
2 cloves garlic, minced

Directions

Toss the broccoli florets with butter, salt and crushed peppercorns until well coated on all sides. Cook in the preheated Air Fryer at 400 degrees F for 6 minutes until they've softened.
In the meantime, make your aioli by mixing the mayo, lemon juice, mustard and garlic in a bowl. Serve the roasted broccoli with the sauce on the side.

Greek zucchini

128 Calories; 1.2g Fat; 6.2g Carbs; 3.9g Protein; 2.7g Sugars

Ingredients

1/2 pound zucchini, cut into thin rounds 1 teaspoon extra-virgin olive oil
1/2 teaspoon dried sage, crushed 1/2 teaspoon oregano
1/4 teaspoon ground bay leaf
Coarse sea salt and ground black pepper, to taste Greek dipping sauce:
1/2 cup Greek yogurt
1/2 teaspoon fresh lemon juice 2 tablespoons mayonnaise
1/2 teaspoon garlic, pressed

Directions

Toss the zucchini rounds with olive oil and spices and place them in the Air Fryer cooking basket.
Cook in the preheated Air Fryer at 400 degrees F for 10 minutes; shaking the basket halfway through the cooking time.
Let it cool slightly and cook an additional minute or so until crispy and golden brown.
Meanwhile, make the sauce by whisking all the sauce ingredients; place the sauce in the refrigerator until ready to serve.
Serve the crispy zucchini rounds with Greek dipping sauce on the side.

Greek Tiganites

384 Calories; 14.1g Fat; 55.2g Carbs; 11.8g Protein; 20.5g Sugars

Ingredients

1/2 cup plain flour 1/2 cup barley flour
1 teaspoon baking powder A pinch of salt
A pinch of sugar
A pinch of cinnamon 1 egg
1/2 cup milk
1/2 cup carbonated water
1 tablespoon butter, melted 3 tablespoons honey
3 tablespoons walnuts, chopped 3 tablespoons Greek yogurt

Directions

Thoroughly combine the flour, baking powder, salt, sugar and cinnamon in a large bowl. Fold in the egg and mix again.
Gradually pour in the milk, water and melted butter, whisking continuously, until well combined. Let the batter stand for about 30 minutes.
Spritz the Air Fryer baking pan with a cooking spray. Pour the batter into the pan using a measuring cup.
Cook at 230 degrees F for 6 to 8 minutes or until golden brown. Repeat with the remaining batter.
Serve your tiganites with the honey, walnuts and Greek yogurt.

Chocolate cake

546 Calories; 34.1g Fat; 55.4g Carbs; 11.4g Protein; 25.7g Sugars

Ingredients

1/2 cup self-rising flour
6 tablespoons brown sugar 5 tablespoons coconut milk 4 tablespoons coconut oil
4 tablespoons unsweetened cocoa powder 2 eggs
A pinch of grated nutmeg A pinch of salt

Directions

Mix all the ingredients together; divide the batter between two mugs. Place the mugs in the Air Fryer cooking basket and cook at 390 degrees F for about 10 minutes.

CPSIA information can be obtained
at www.ICGtesting.com
Printed in the USA
BVHW080020190521
607637BV00004B/571

9 781802 750836